THE Carrot
AND OTHER ROOT VEGETABLES

Millicent E. Selsam

photographs by Jerome Wexler

WILLIAM MORROW AND COMPANY
NEW YORK

Text copyright © 1971 by Millicent E. Selsam
Photographs copyright © 1971 by Jerome Wexler
All rights reserved. No part of this book may be reproduced
or utilized in any form or by any means, electronic or mechanical,
including photocopying, recording or by any information
storage and retrieval system, without permission in writing
from the Publisher. Inquiries should be addressed to
William Morrow and Company, Inc.,
105 Madison Ave., New York, N.Y. 10016.
Printed in the United States of America.
Library of Congress Catalog Card Number 70-155994
Design by Cynthia Basil
1   2   3   4   5   75   74   73   72   71

By the Same Author

ANIMALS AS PARENTS

THE COURTSHIP OF ANIMALS

HOW ANIMALS LIVE TOGETHER

HOW ANIMALS TELL TIME

HOW TO GROW HOUSE PLANTS

THE LANGUAGE OF ANIMALS

MAPLE TREE

MICROBES AT WORK

MILKWEED

PEANUT

PLANTS THAT HEAL

PLANTS THAT MOVE

THE PLANTS WE EAT

PLAY WITH PLANTS

PLAY WITH SEEDS

PLAY WITH TREES

THE TOMATO AND OTHER FRUIT VEGETABLES

UNDERWATER ZOOS

The author and photographer thank
Miss Frances Miner,
Curator of Instruction, Brooklyn Botanic Garden,
for checking the text and photographs of this book.

Acknowledgments for Photographs

D. M. Compton, National Audubon Society, 45
United States Department of Agriculture, 4, 5, 26–27, 44
United States Department of Agriculture-Soil Conservation Service, 25
Jeanne White, National Audubon Society, 18

Small seeds like those above
can grow into big carrots.

COTYLEDONS

First a carrot seed sprouts.

Two long, narrow seed
leaves, or cotyledons,
come out of the seed.
The cotyledons have food
stored in them. The
young carrot plant uses
this food as it grows.

6

Here you can see the first true carrot leaf.

If you gently pull the carrot out of the ground, you can see a long, thin root. Usually carrots are not dug at this stage. They are left in the soil, and they keep growing.

New leaves grow out on top. This carrot plant is a type called Tiny Sweet. It grows to full size in a flowerpot.

The leaves manufacture food for the
growing plant. But they make a lot more
than the plant needs to live and grow.
The extra food moves down to the
underground root, where it is stored.
The root grows thicker and longer.

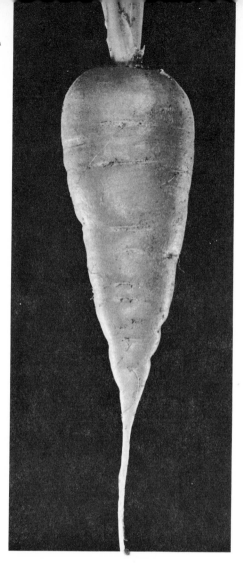

Here it looks like the
carrot root we eat.
At this time farmers dig
the carrots out of the
ground, and they are sold
in the vegetable markets.

11

When the carrot is in the ground, before it is pulled up, there are smaller white roots growing out of it. When the carrot is harvested, the roots are broken off and left in the ground. In this picture, the soil has been washed away carefully, so that you can see these roots.

Look at a carrot. You can find the places where the fine roots were attached to it.

When carrots are dug out of the ground, the tops of the plant are just stems and leaves. Next year the farmer will want to grow more carrots. But he will need seeds to plant. Where does he get them from?

All seeds come from flowers.
But so far the carrot has
not produced any flowers.
Seed farms grow a special
crop of carrots. The farmer
picks the best-looking ones
and plants them in the ground
again. The upper part
of the carrot is really stem
tissue and can produce buds.
These buds grow out into
new stems and leaves.

Here a carrot like the ones grown at the seed farms is planted in a flowerpot. The leaves look like those of the carrots grown from seed. But this time the carrot develops differently. Special stems produce flowers. Do these carrot flowers look familiar?

16

They may remind you of Queen Anne's lace, a relative of the carrot. Its lacy flowers, which look like umbrellas, are much the same as carrot flowers. But its root is not like the carrot root. It is tough and woody, so it is not good to eat.

If you look underneath a carrot flower, you can see that it is really a collection of little clusters of flowers. This flower head is called an "umbel," because the stalks come out from the same point like the spokes of an umbrella.

In this picture you can see one tiny cluster of flowers removed from the big flower head.

In this picture there is one single flower.
Two stamens stick out from the flower.
Usually there are five stamens, but three
of them have fallen off. At the top of each
stamen there is a sac of pollen grains.

Notice the ovary below the petals.
It is the bottom part of the pistil.

Here the petals are removed, and you can see the entire pistil. The top part is divided into two sections called "styles." At the tip of each style there is a part called a "stigma," which has a sticky surface. Inside the spiny ovary there are two ovules, which can change into seeds if they are fertilized. Right on top of the ovary there is a ring of juicy tissue that manufactures nectar, a sweet liquid.

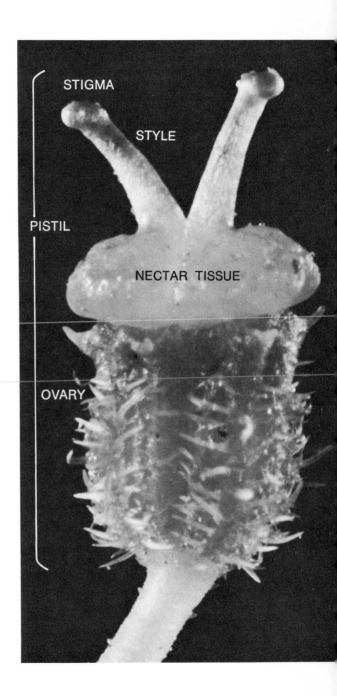

21

Insects come to suck the nectar. They
get dusted with pollen, and accidentally
they carry pollen from flower to flower.

When the pollen lands on the sticky stigma, it
sends out a tube that grows down to the ovary,
where the ovules are. The contents of each
pollen tube join with an ovule. Now the ovules
are fertilized and can change into seeds.

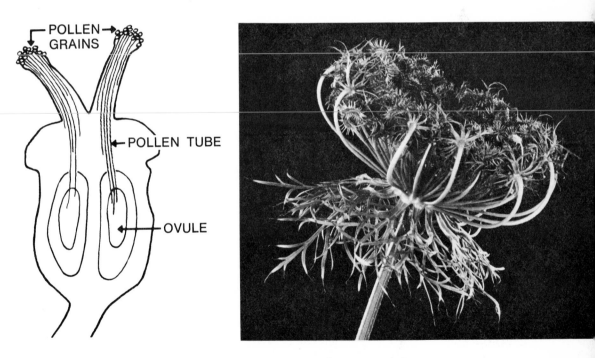

After fertilization, the flowers on the outside
bend inward. The umbel looks like a bird's nest.

23

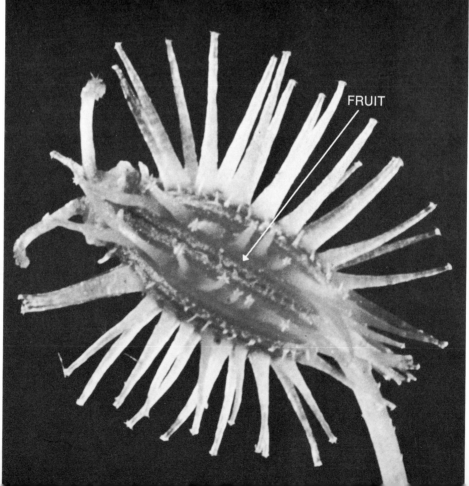

FRUIT

Meanwhile, the seeds mature and the ovary around
them becomes prickly. As is true of all plants,
the part that contains seeds is called a fruit.
Thus, the ovary of the carrot develops into a prickly
fruit. There are two seeds in each prickly fruit.

This picture shows a large field of carrots going to
seed. The spiny fruits stick together. Farmers have
to use machines to rub off the spines and separate
the seeds before they put the seeds into packages.

Like carrots,
radishes are roots.

A radish seed is sprouting.
The little root hairs make the
root look like a bottle brush.

Leaves form.

28

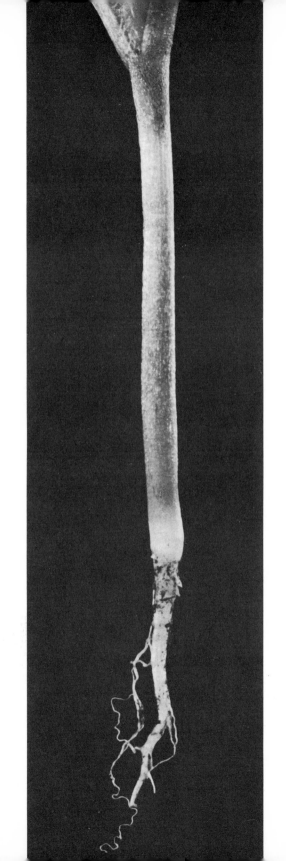

But there is no radish
under the ground yet.

29

Now the radish root begins to
swell, because extra food is
being stored in it. The root
grows bigger. At last it is ready
to be pulled out of the ground.

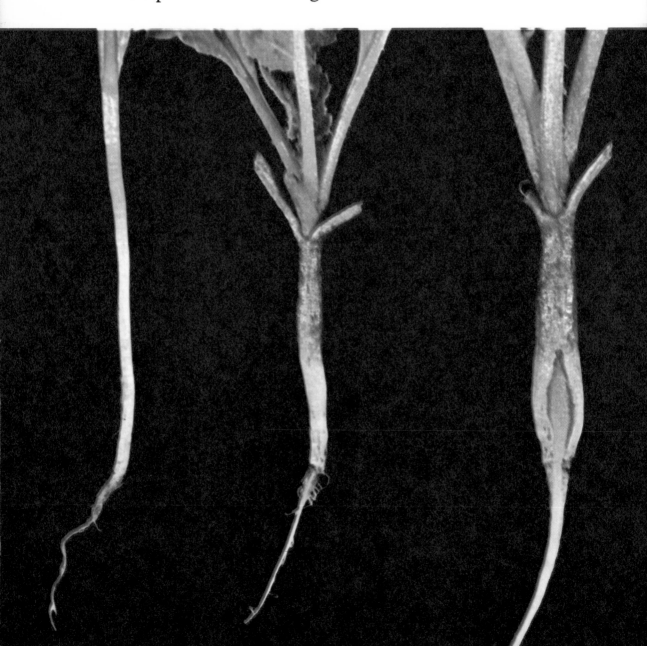

If radish seed is planted in the spring, radish plants grow, produce flowers, and set seed during the summer. If seed is planted in the fall, flowers do not form until the following spring.

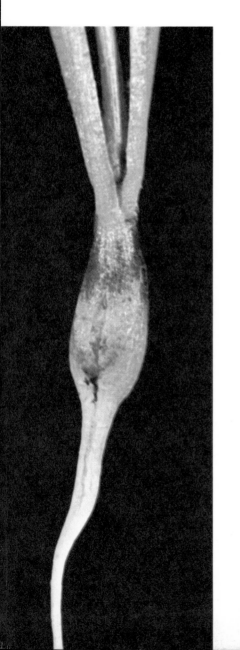

Insects carry pollen from one flower to another.
After the pollen tubes grow down to the ovary
and fertilize the ovules, the ovaries change to
fruits and the ovules change to seeds.

The long, thin pods in these pictures are
radish fruits. You can see the seeds inside.

Turnips grow like carrots.
The first year the turnip
root gets bigger and
bigger while only leaves
form above the ground.

The turnips are harvested
at this stage. To get turnip
seed, however, the best
turnips are picked, stored,
and planted in the spring.

When the turnip
grows the second
time, leaves form
again, but now
flowers appear.

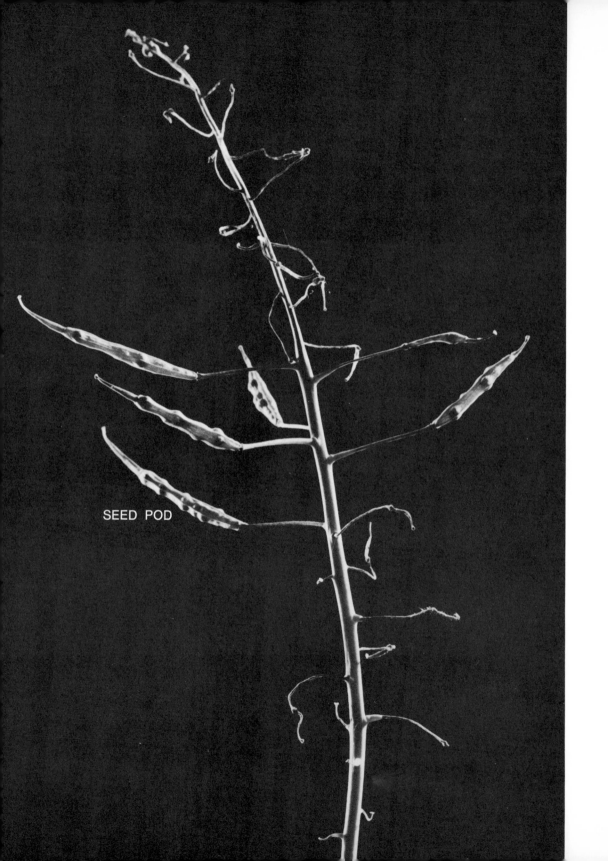

SEED POD

Only those flowers
that receive pollen
and are fertilized can
produce seed pods.

In the picture at
right, a pod is
opening and you can
see the turnip seeds.

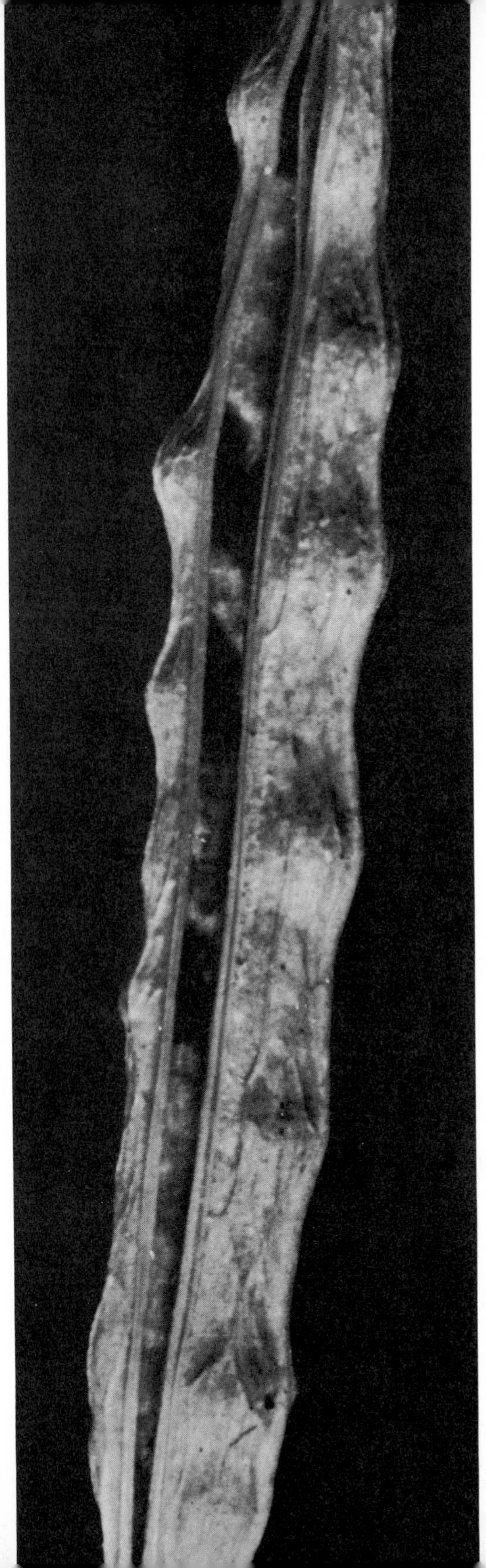

37

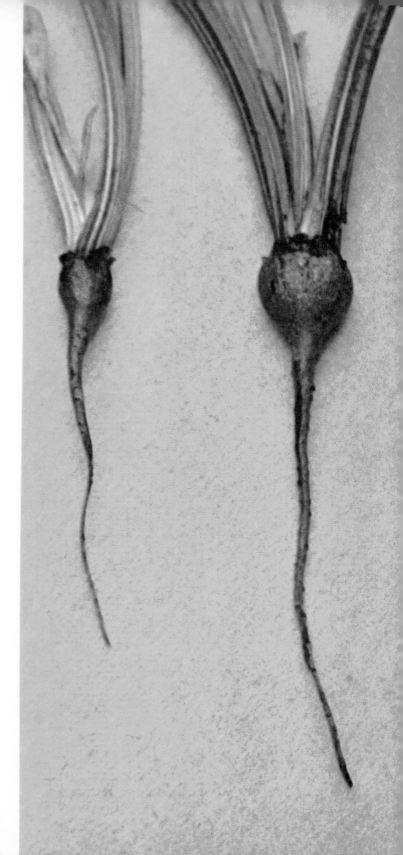

Beets grow
like carrots
and turnips.
The first year
the underground
beet root forms.

38

Here is what a beet
plant looks like at
the end of the first
year's growth.
Farmers harvest
beets at this stage.

FLOWERS

To get seeds, the best beets are picked, kept in cold storage over the winter, and planted in the spring. As is true of all root plants, the top part of the beet is part of the stem and has buds. The second year the plant grows, both leaves and flowers form.

41

FLOWERS

The flowers are
tiny and clustered
together at the base
of small leaves.

Each ovary has one ovule. After fertilization, the ovaries of several small flowers fuse together. Thus they form a seed ball of several seeds, one from each flower. These seed balls are planted in the ground the following spring.

Sweet potatoes are another root vegetable.
Sweet potato vines sprawl over the
ground. No flowers or seeds are produced
in the north temperate zone. Sweet potatoes
flower and set seed only in the tropics.

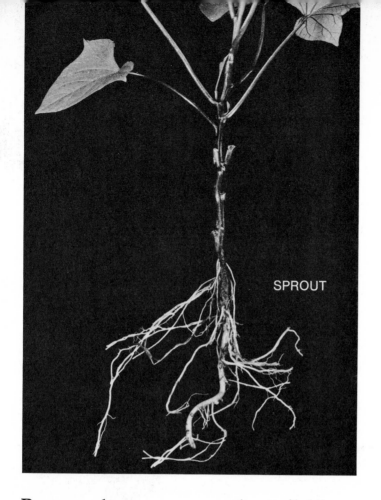

SPROUT

Because there are no seeds available, sweet potatoes are raised from other sweet-potato roots. Medium-sized roots are put into special beds of warm soil. When sprouts appear on the roots, they are pulled off and set out in the fields.

As the new plant grows, sweet-potato roots form under the ground.

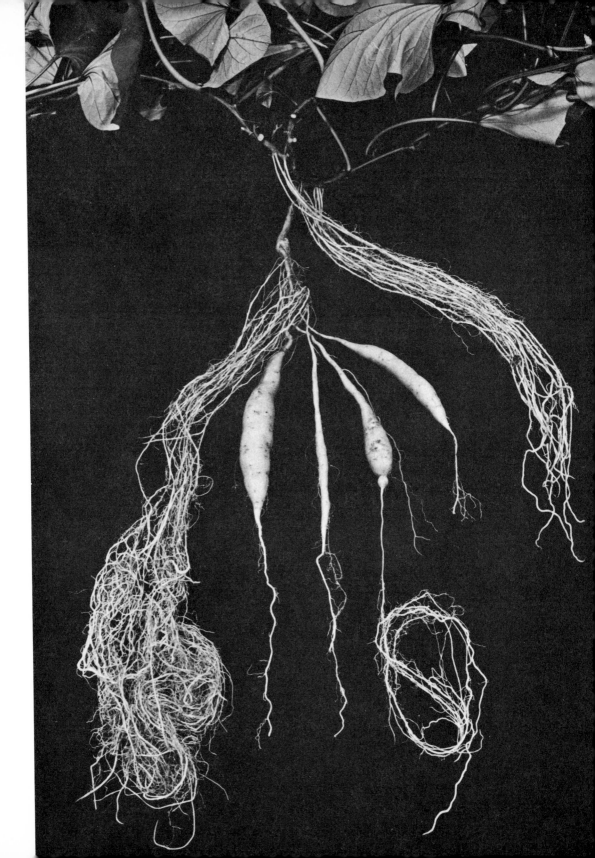

Carrots, turnips, and beets are called "biennials." Radishes act as biennials if they are planted in the fall.

Biennials take two years to complete their life cycle. The first year they store up food in the roots we eat. If these roots are left in the ground or pulled up and planted again, they produce flowers and set seed during the second year of their growth.

The sweet-potato vine is called a "perennial." It continues its growth from year to year. Many other plants, like the radishes planted in the spring, are called "annuals." They complete their life cycle from seed to seed in one year.

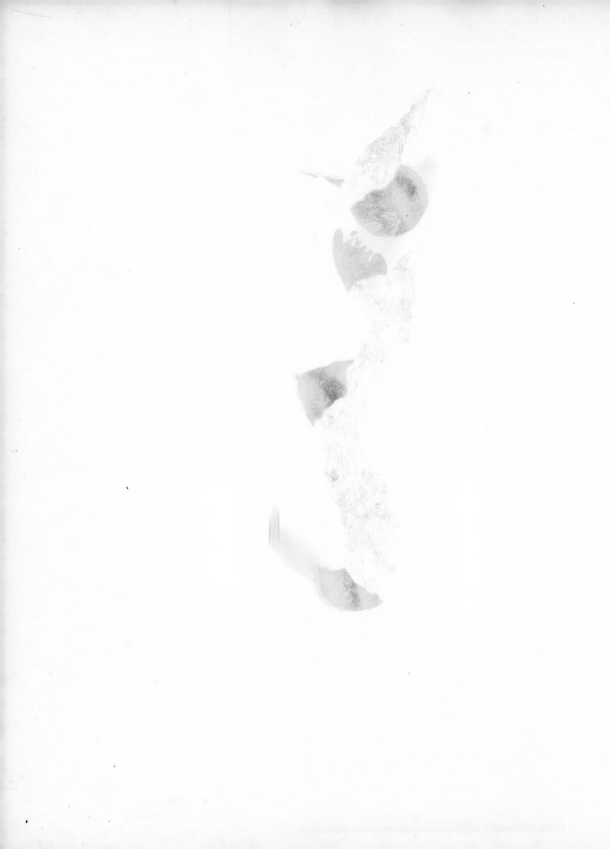